The Gift of
GOLDENS

The Gift of
GOLDENS

WILLOW CREEK PRESS

Published by Willow Creek Press, Inc.
P.O. Box 147, Minocqua, Wisconsin 54548

Photo Credits:

p7 © Superstock/age fotostock; p8 © Juniors Bildarchiv/age fotostock; p11 © Juniors Bildarchiv/age fotostock; p12 © Jessica Sladek/agefotostock; p15 © FLPA/Angela Hampton/age fotostock; p16 © Juniors Bildarchiv/age fotostock; p19 © De Meester Johan/age fotostock; p20 © Martin Valigursky/agefotostock; p23 © Juniors Bildarchiv/age fotostock; p24 © Juniors Bildarchiv/age fotostock; p27 © Juniors Bildarchiv/age fotostock; p28 © Juniors Bildarchiv/age fotostock; p31 © De Meester Johan/age fotostock; p32 © Jim McGuire/age fotostock; p35 © Juniors Bildarchiv/age fotostock; p36 © Carmen Nasarre/age fotostock; p39 © Juniors Bildarchiv/age fotostock; p40 © Bryan Mullennix/age fotostock; p43 © Fotosearch RM/age fotostock; p44 © Juniors Bildarchiv/age fotostock; p47 © Juniors Bildarchiv/age fotostock; p48 © stockbrokerxtra/age fotostock; p51 © Juniors Bildarchiv/age fotostock; p52 © Richard Semik/age fotostock; p55 © Stefanie Krause-Wiecz/age fotostock; p56 © Martin Valigursky/age fotostock; p59 © Stefanie Krause-Wiecz/age fotostock; p60 © Corbis/age fotostock; p63 © Juniors Bildarchiv/age fotostock; p64 © stockbrokerxtra/age fotostock; p67 © Martin Valigursky/age fotostock; p68 © Frank Siteman/age fotostock; p71 © Juniors Bildarchiv/age fotostock; p76 © Stefanie Krause-Wiecz/age fotostock; p79 © ARCO/De Meester/age fotostock; p80 © Juniors Bildarchiv/age fotostock; p83 © Juan Muñoz/age fotostock; p84 © Juniors Bildarchiv/age fotostock; p87 © Juniors Bildarchiv/age fotostock; p88 © Helene Rogers/age fotostock; p91 © Juniors Bildarchiv/age fotostock; p92 © Skip Dean/age fotostock; p95 © Roberto Della Vite/age fotostock; p96 © Juniors Bildarchiv/age fotostock;

Design: Donnie Rubo
Printed in China

Some days you're the dog, some days you're the hydrant.
—*Unknown*

ACCEPTANCE

Yesterday I was a dog. Today I'm a dog. Tomorrow I'll probably still be a dog. Sigh! There's so little hope for advancement.
—*Snoopy*

The only valid excuse for not exercising is paralysis.

—*Moira Nordholt*

ATHLETICISM

If you cannot do great things, do small things in a great way.

—*Napoleon Hill*

Fortune befriends the bold.

—John Dryden

BRAVERY

Courage is resistance to fear, mastery
of fear—not absence of fear. Except
a creature be part coward it is not
a compliment to say it is brave.

—Mark Twain

Keep your spirits up. Good things will come
to you and you will come to good things.

—*Glorie Abelhas*

CHEERFULNESS

Wherever you go, no matter what the weather,
always bring your own sunshine.

—*Anthony J. D'Angelo*

Contentment is natural wealth, luxury is artificial poverty.

—*Socrates*

CONTENTMENT

My riches consist not in the extent of my possessions,
but in the fewness of my wants.

—*J. Brotherton*

The cure for boredom is curiosity.
There is no cure for curiosity.

—*Dorothy Parker*

CURIOSITY

Curiosity is little more than
another name for Hope.

—*Augustus William Hare*

Faithfulness and sincerity are the highest things.

—*Confucius*

DEVOTION

Faithfulness lives where love is stronger than instinct.

—*Paul Carvel*

I arise full of eagerness and energy, knowing
well what achievement lies ahead of me.

—*Zane Grey*

ENTHUSIASM

Enthusiasm is the sparkle in your
eyes, the swing in your gait... the
irresistible surge of will and energy.

—*Henry Ford*

Let us not pray to be sheltered from dangers,
but to be fearless when facing them.
—*Rabindranath Tagore*

FEARLESS

To be fearless yet free from hate is a state of
being to which we should all strive
—*Unknown*

Love thy neighbor, and if it requires that you bend your understanding of the truth, the Truth will understand.

—*Robert Brault*

FRIENDLY

I always prefer to believe the best of everybody. It saves so much trouble.

—*Rudyard Kipling*

This life is not for complaint, but for satisfaction.

—*Henry David Thoreau*

FULFILLMENT

Occasionally in life there are those moments of unutterable fulfillment which cannot be completely explained by those symbols called words. Their meanings can only be articulated by the inaudible language of the heart.

—*Martin Luther King, Jr.*

Only the weak are cruel. Gentleness can
only be expected from the strong.

—*Leo F. Buscaglia*

GENTLENESS

There never was any heart truly great and generous,
that was not also tender and compassionate.

—*Robert Frost*

Happiness is not a matter of intensity but of
balance, order, rhythm and harmony.

—*Thomas Merton*

HARMONY

Just because man no longer understands
his place in the universe, don't let
him assume all God's creatures have
become equally confused and trivial.

—*Bill Tarrant*

In about the same degree as you are helpful, you will be happy.

—*Karl Reiland*

HELPFUL

Being good is commendable, but only when it is
combined with doing good is it useful.

—*Unknown*

Sometimes "What the hell?" is the
best answer to the question.

—*Unknown*

IMPULSIVE

Reason only controls us after emotion and
impulse have lost their impetus.

—*Carlton Simon*

The perfection of a life with a dog, like the perfection of an autumn, is disturbing because you know, even as it begins, that it must end. Time bestows the gift and steals it in the process.

—*George Bird Evans*

INEVITABILITY

A good dog never dies. He always stays. He walks beside you on crisp autumn days when frost is on the fields and winter's drawing near, his head is within our hand in his old way.

—*Mary Carolyn Davies*

I am neither especially clever nor especially gifted, only very, very curious

—*Albert Einstein*

INQUISITIVE

The one real object of education is to be in the condition of continually asking questions.

—*Bishop Mandell Creighton*

You sometimes cannot ask to have your own way, instead you must insist on it.

—*Unknown*

INSISTENT

Dogs feel very strongly that they should always go with you in the car, in case the need should arise for them to bark violently at nothing right in your ear.

—*Dave Barry*

The aspects of things that are most important for us are hidden because of their simplicity and familiarity.

—*Ludwig Wittgenstein*

INTIMACY

It requires the intimacy of daily living with a dog to know the subtle quality of his mind, the ham-smell of his ears, and that his wet nose in your mouth tastes salty.

—*George Bird Evans*

In order to make us covet a thing, it is only necessary to make the thing difficult to obtain.
—*Mark Twain*

JEALOUSY

Envy is the art of counting the other fellow's blessings instead of your own.
—*Harold Coffin*

It's nice to be important, but it's more important to be nice.

—*Unknown*

KINDNESS

She had always been kind. Sometimes, however, she wondered if she was appreciated. "Even so," she thought, "I shall always smile and be kind." Once a Golden Retriever, always a Golden Retriever.

—*Charles Schultz*

A dog is the only thing on earth that loves
you more than he loves himself.

—*Josh Billings*

LOYALTY

Don't ask me to leave you and turn back. I
will go where you go and live where you live.

—*the Bible*

You have to expect things of yourself before you can do them.

—*Michael Jordan*

MOTIVATED

Believe in yourself! Have faith in your abilities! Without a humble but reasonable confidence in your own powers you cannot be successful or happy.

—*Norman Vincent Peale*

A day without a nap is like a cupcake without frosting.
—Terri Guillemets

NAP TIME

I count it as a certainty that in paradise, everyone naps.
—Tom Hodgkinson

Whenever there is authority, there is a natural inclination to disobedience.

—*Thomas C. Haliburton*

NAUGHTY

It's no use growing older if you only learn new ways of misbehaving yourself.

—*Hector Hugh Munro*

True nobility is exempt from fear.

—*Marcus Tullius Cicero*

NOBLE

Grave eyes, grave bearing, dignity of kings; The gentleness and trust as of a child; The flawless poise that veils old savage things. But half-remembered from the vanished wild.

—*C.T. Davis*

It is for each of us freely to choose whom we shall serve, and find in that obedience our freedom.

—*Mary Richards*

OBEDIENCE

Teachability and trust always leads to total obedience.

—*Ed Townsend*

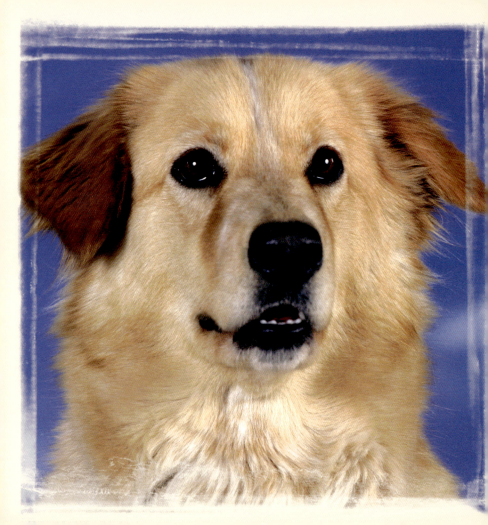

If your dog doesn't like someone, you probably shouldn't either.

—*Unknown*

OBSERVANT

If you think dogs can't count, try putting three biscuits in your pocket and then giving Fido only two of them.

—*Phil Pastoret*

Nothing is so often irretrievably missed as a daily opportunity.

—*Mari von Ebner-Eschenbach*

OPPORTUNISTIC

Realize that ultimate success comes from opportunistic,
bold move which, by definition, cannot be planned.

—*Ross Johnson*

The bond with a true dog is as lasting
as the ties of this earth will ever be.

—*Konrad Lorenz*

PARTNERS

He is your friend, your partner, your
defender, your dog. You are his life, his
love, his leader. He will be yours, faithful
and true, to the last beat of his heart.
You owe it to him to be worthy
of such devotion.

—*Unknown*

Each one has to find his peace from within. And peace to be real must be unaffected by outside circumstances.

—*Mahatma Gandi*

PEACE

Boredom is the feeling that everything is a waste of time; serenity, that nothing is.

—*Thomas S. Szasz*

Never give up. Never give up, never, never, never, never.

—*Winston Churchill*

PERSISTENT

Perseverance and persistence in spite of all obstacles: It is this, that in all things distinguishes the strong soul from the weak.

—*Thomas Carlyle*

Live and work but do not forget to play, to
have fun in life and really enjoy it.

—*Eileen Caddy*

PLAYFUL

We are never more fully alive,
more completely ourselves, or
more deeply engrossed in anything
than when we are playing.

—*Charles Schaefer*

Sometimes questions are more important than the answers.

—*Nancy Willard*

QUESTIONING

Learn from yesterday, live for today, hope for tomorrow.
The important thing is not to stop questioning.

—*Albert Einstein*

There is no sincerer love
than the love of food.
—*George Bernard Shaw*

RAVENOUS

One of the very nicest things about
life is the way we must regularly
stop whatever it is we are doing and
devote our attention to eating.
—*Luciano Pavarotti*

Repentance is not so much remorse for what we have done as the fear of the consequences.

—Francois de la Rochefoucauld

REPENTANT

Don't be angry with me for long, and don't lock me up as punishment. You have your work, entertainment and friends. I only have you.

—Unknown

The deed is everything, the glory is naught.
—*Johann Wolfgang von Goethe*

SERVICE

I am only one, but I am one. I cannot do everything, but I can do something. And I will not let what I cannot do interfere with what I can do.
—*Edward Everett Hale.*

Be content with what you have, rejoice in the way things are. When you realize there is nothing lacking, the whole world belongs to you.

—*Lao Tzu*

SIMPLICITY

They do not for all their marvelous instincts appear to know about death. Being such wonderfully uncomplicated beings, they need us to do their worrying.

—*George Bird Evans*

When you come to the end of your rope, tie a knot and hang on.

—*Franklin D. Roosevelt*

STUBBORNNESS

Stubbornly persist, and you will find that the limits of your stubbornness go well beyond the stubbornness of your limits.

—*Robert Brault*

The trouble with resisting temptation is it may never come your way again.

—*Korman's Law*

TEMPTATION

There is a charm about the forbidden that makes it unspeakably desirable.

—*Mark Twain*

When you find peace within yourself,
you can live at peace with others.

—*Unknown*

TOLERANT

Forbearance is the root of quietness
and assurance forever.

—*Ieyasu Tokugawa*

Life is one grand, sweet song, so start the music.

—*Ronald Reagan*

VOCAL

If you're quiet, you're not living. You've
got to be noisy, colorful and lively.

—*Mel Brooks*

The most affectionate creature in the world is a wet dog.

—*Ambrose Bierce*

WATERPROOFED

To do anything truly worth doing, I must not stand back shivering and thinking of the cold and danger, but jump in with gusto and scramble through as well as I can.

—*Og Mandino*

How old would you be if you didn't
know how old you are?

—*Satchel Paige*

YOUTHFUL

We don't stop playing because we grow old;
we grow old because we stop playing.

—*George Bernard Shaw*

Today is life—the only life you are sure of. Make the most of today. Let the winds of enthusiasm sweep through you.

–Dale Carnegie

ZEST

Dance as though no one is watching you; love as though you have never been hurt before, sing as though no one can hear you, live as though heaven is on earth.

—Alfred Souza